HEINEMANN Profiles

Charles Rennie Mackintosh

Richard Tames

First published in Great Britain by Heinemann
Library, Halley Court, Jordan Hill, Oxford
OX2 8EJ, a division of Reed Educational and
Professional Publishing Ltd.
Heinemann is a registered trademark of Reed
Educational & Professional Publishing Limited.

OXFORD MELBOURNE AUCKLAND
JOHANNESBURG BLANTYRE
GABORONE IBADAN PORTSMOUTH
NH (USA) CHICAGO

Designed by Visual Image
Originated by Dot Gradations
Printed and bound in Hong Kong/China

04 03 02 01 00
10 9 8 7 6 5 4 3 2 1

ISBN 0 431 08633 8

**British Library Cataloguing
in Publication Data**

Tames, Richard, 1946-
Charles Rennie Mackintosh. –
   (Heinemann Profiles)
1. Mackintosh, Charles Rennie, 1868–1928
   – Juvenile literature 2. Artists – Scotland
   – Biography – Juvenile literature
I. Title
709.2
ISBN 0431086338

Acknowledgements
The Publishers would like to thank the following
for permission to reproduce photographs: T & R
Annan & Sons Ltd: pp5, 18, 19, 33; Glasgow
Museums: pp36, 39; Glasgow School of Art
Collection: pp11, 15, 22, 23, 32, 40, 42, 43, 47;
Hunterian Art Gallery, University of Glasgow:
pp8, 10, 12, 24, 35, 38; Manchester Central
Libraries: p26; Popperfoto: p7; Scotland in Focus:
D Corrance pp4, 16, 44, 49, A G Firth pp9, 27,
29, I McLean p20, R Schofield pp17, 31, 51.

Cover photograph reproduced with permission of
T & R Annan & Sons Ltd.

Every effort has been made to contact copyright
holders of any material reproduced in this book.
Any omissions will be rectified in subsequent
printings if notice is given to the Publisher.

For more information about Heinemann Library
books, or to order, please phone ++44 (0)1865
888066, or send a fax to ++44 (0)1865 314091.
You can visit our website at
www.heinemann.co.uk.

Any words appearing in the text in bold, **like
this**, are explained in the Glossary.

CONTENTS

WHO WAS CHARLES RENNIE MACKINTOSH ?

Oak bedroom chair designed for The Hill House 1903.

Look for a book about Charles Rennie Mackintosh in a library and it will probably be shelved under '**architecture**'. But Mackintosh thought of himself as an artist. Many people nowadays think of him as an interior decorator and designer. In his short working life he designed over 400 pieces of furniture but completed only about a dozen buildings. Much of his time and talent was spent on alterations to buildings which already existed, or on preparing designs for projects which never happened. For the last ten years of his life he devoted himself to painting **watercolours**, and only just managed to earn a living by designing **textiles**.

A ROLLER-COASTER REPUTATION

Mackintosh's career began in obscurity and ended in failure. But for a brief period of little more than a decade he was hailed as one of the most exciting talents in Europe. Almost all of Mackintosh's work was

done in or around his native city of Glasgow, in
Scotland, but his designs were applauded and
imitated from Belgium to Hungary – though in
England he remained virtually unknown.

The last fifteen years of Mackintosh's life should
have seen him at the height of success. But, by the
time Mackintosh died at the age of 60, he had been
all but forgotten. The furniture, drawings and
paintings he left behind were officially valued as
virtually worthless. Had Mackintosh lived another
60 years, however, he would have seen a desk he
designed fetch the highest-ever price paid at auction
for an item of twentieth-century furniture.

BACKGROUND AND BOYHOOD

Charles Rennie Mackintosh, the fourth of eleven children, was born into an ordinary, respectable family in 1868. His father was a policeman and a keen gardener. The Mackintosh home, a three-roomed **tenement** flat in the oldest part of Glasgow, was always full of flowers.

When Mackintosh was six years old the family moved into a five-room house, in the **suburbs**. The house overlooked a vast cemetery, filled with

Glasgow – no mean city

Mackintosh was born, educated and found fame in one of the boom cities of the nineteenth century. By 1901 Glasgow was not only by far the largest city in Scotland but also the 'second city of the **British Empire**'. Its expansion was based on modern industries such as cotton, chemicals, engineering and, above all, shipbuilding. Glaswegians were rightly proud of their city and used their prosperity to support **civic** projects such as laying out Kelvingrove Park and constructing magnificent new **Gothic** buildings for the ancient university. In such a thriving city ambitious architects, artists and designers could see opportunities for work all around them.

elaborately carved tombs and monuments. Mackintosh passed it every day on his way to school and played there afterwards. As a schoolboy he had great problems with reading and spelling but showed an early talent for drawing. Mackintosh also developed a limp, caused by a **contracted sinew** in one foot. This disability made an office job desirable, rather than one which involved physical work, and at sixteen he started work with the architect John Hutchison.

Much of Glasgow's prosperity was built on the shipbuilding industry.

A STAR STUDENT

After his day in the office Mackintosh went to evening classes at Glasgow School of Art. He worked hard at drawing, passed examinations and won prizes. He also studied **architecture** and was encouraged to enter designs for the annual National Competition of the Department of Science and Art. Francis Newbery, the School's new head, recognized Mackintosh as an outstanding student.

Mackintosh's design for an art school diploma uses the stretched, curving shapes he later applied to furniture and buildings.

In 1888, at the age of 20, Mackintosh was awarded a prize by the Glasgow Institute of Fine Arts for a design for a terraced house. In the same year he was paid for his first piece of professional work as a designer – a gravestone for Chief Constable Andrew McCall. Having a policeman for a father and a graveyard for a view had unexpected advantages.

Glasgow's architecture included both Gothic and Classical styles.

THE ARCHITECT AS ARTIST

In 1889 Mackintosh completed his **pupilage** and left John Hutchison to join Glasgow's fourth largest architectural **practice**, Honeyman and Keppie. Honeyman was 58, cultured and experienced. Keppie was only 27, a better organizer than designer, but brought much-needed cash into the business. Four-fifths of all the firm's projects were alterations or extensions, rather than **commissions** for brand-new buildings. This meant that there were few opportunities for Mackintosh to reveal his very individual talent.

Compare this sketch with the staircase towers shown on page 27.

MAKING A NAME

In 1890 Mackintosh's design for a public meeting hall won him a travelling studentship, offered in memory of Glasgow architect Alexander Thomson. The £60 prize paid for three months sketching in Italy. The following year Mackintosh lectured on Scottish **baronial architecture**, arguing that it was Scotland's national style, based on the **fortified** houses of the turbulent sixteenth and seventeenth centuries.

Mackintosh
among 'The
Immortals'.
Margaret
Macdonald
stands at the
far right.

Outside office hours Mackintosh continued to enter design competitions. He also gave more public lectures and began to dress like an artist, wearing a floppy bow-tie and sporting a dashing, pointed moustache.

NEW FRIENDS, NEW INTERESTS

In 1891 Mackintosh and his best friend, fellow **draughtsman** Herbert McNair, met a group of women students who called themselves 'The **Immortals**'. The group included two sisters, Frances and Margaret Macdonald, who soon joined Mackintosh and McNair to become 'The Four'. Inspired by **Celtic myths** they produced paintings of willowy women and contorted trees in eerie twilight settings. Critics thought their work clever but weird, and called them 'The Spook School'.

PROFESSIONAL LANDMARKS, PRIVATE PASTIMES

This design combines circles and flowing curves in a balanced geometry.

As a junior **draughtsman** Mackintosh worked on projects controlled by senior colleagues, providing decorative details at Craigie Hall and Glasgow Art Club. He got his first big job, designing a rear extension for the *Glasgow Herald* building, in 1893. Its angular corner water-tower (a precaution against printing-room fires) is a clear echo of the Scottish baronial style, which featured overhanging turrets called bartizans. In 1895 he helped design Martyrs' Public School, to be built on the very street where he was born. Its unusual roof-timbers look distinctly Japanese – a new influence on art and design at that time.

In his spare time Mackintosh began to design wooden furniture and, as one of 'The Four', helped design **controversial** posters. Gleeson White, editor of *The Studio*, defended his work on the grounds that, although 'Mr Mackintosh's posters may be somewhat trying to the average person', they were wonderfully decorative – and did grab the attention of the passer-by, which is just what a poster is supposed to do.

The Glasgow Herald building – like a Scottish fortress in brick.

FAME AT LAST

1896 marked the turning-point in Mackintosh's life. He was invited to exhibit at the Arts and Crafts Exhibition Society's annual London show. He met Hermann Muthesius, a German architect and diplomat who was to be his greatest **champion**. He was introduced to Miss Kate Cranston, his best **patron**. And he won a competition to design a new home for the Glasgow School of Art, where he had so recently been a student.

MISS CRANSTON

Kate Cranston, sister of a Glasgow tea-merchant, was a firm believer that alcohol – the 'demon drink' – was a curse on Scotland. As an alternative to Glasgow's hundreds of public houses, she built up a chain of tea rooms, offering light meals, excellent service and elegant surroundings, where people could meet, chat, refresh themselves, read newspapers or play chess, dominoes or billiards. Miss Cranston realized that daring **decor** could be a talking-point for her customers and in 1896 **commissioned** the **controversial** Mackintosh to decorate the walls of the lunch room at her Buchanan Street premises. Two years later she asked him to design furniture as part of the make-over of her first branch, on Argyle Street.

THE SCHOOL OF ART

Francis ('Fra') Newbery was determined that Glasgow's School of Art should have a new home to match those of Birmingham or Manchester, its nearest rivals. In 1896 Honeyman and Keppie were invited to enter the design competition. What they submitted was Mackintosh's work but the formal credit went to Keppie, because he was the supervising **partner**.

Elongated female figures framed in drapery were a characteristic Mackintosh **motif**.

Mackintosh's masterpiece was built on a steeply sloping site, which meant that it had three storeys on one side and five on the other. It incorporated two dozen different types of studio and classroom, plus offices, meeting rooms, lecture theatres, common rooms, store areas, etc. At first glance a bold, bare building, it is in fact full of decorative detail. Light and spacious inside, it also meets the practical needs of teachers and students alike. The delicately curved iron window-brackets ingeniously double as supports for window-cleaners' planks. But many features were just for effect. The tower beside the entrance is higher than the staircase inside it. And the balcony over the entrance is useless for seeing the fine view – which is on the other side.

The Glasgow School of Art.

Bold straight lines are offset with delicate curving details.

OTHER TRIUMPHS

By the time the School of Art opened in 1899, Mackintosh had also completed Queen's Cross Church and hall at Springbank and the Free Church Halls at Ruchill Street. In 1897 Mackintosh and the Macdonald sisters were profiled in *The Studio* and mentioned in the first issue of a German art magazine, *Dekorative Kunst* (Decorative Art), whose publisher **commissioned** Mackintosh to design dining-room furniture. A Glasgow publisher, Robert Maclehose, ordered a bedroom.

In 1898 Mackintosh's partners set him to produce the firm's entries for competitions for a National Bank of Scotland headquarters and for the **pavilions** of a Glasgow International Exhibition to be held in 1901. Neither of these designs won but they showed that his seniors at last recognized his professionalism and talent.

MARRIAGE AND MARGARET

'The Four' ended as two twos. In 1899 Herbert McNair married Frances Macdonald and moved to Liverpool to teach decorative design. Mackintosh married Margaret Macdonald in 1900, and they settled in Glasgow.

Margaret Macdonald – a partner in art as well as marriage.

A HOME OF THEIR OWN

The Mackintoshes' first home was a flat. Only photographs survive to show how it set the basic pattern for their later work as decorators. The spacious rooms were kept uncluttered, except for a carefully positioned flower arrangement or a small group of pots. Even their Persian cats had their own cushions, either side of the fireplace. Walls, floors and ceilings were kept plain, as a backdrop to the few pieces of furniture which, like the light-fittings, were individually designed. The materials used for decorating were often unusual: coarse brown wrapping-paper on the dining-room walls; hard-wearing sailcloth, **stencilled** with a chequerboard pattern, on the stairs. Small panels of cheap **enamel** and coloured glass were used to catch the light with jewel-like gleams. The Mackintoshes' home was not

The drawing-room of the Mackintoshes' first home at 120 Mains Street.

meant to display wealth but art and taste. The overall effect was both striking and restful.

INDEPENDENT PROJECTS

Mackintosh's first independent architectural work was a home for Glasgow provisions merchant, William Davidson. The site, at Kilmacolm, gave the house its name – Windyhill. Mackintosh's design was suitably rugged, like a rambling Scottish **fortified** manor-house, built of rubble and faced with **roughcast**, called harling in Scotland. L-shaped in plan, the living rooms were ranged along the long arm of the L, the kitchen, laundry, etc. in the short arm. Davidson's neighbours thought Windyhill looked like a prison but the Davidsons remained warm admirers of Mackintosh's work.

Hill House, Helensburgh, built for the Glasgow publisher Walter Blackie between 1902 and 1904, was a luxurious version of Windyhill, costing over twice as much. Based on the same L-shaped plan and also surfaced with harling, the house had over two dozen rooms and 58 windows of 40 different shapes, sizes or materials.

Hill House seen from the south-east.

Mackintosh's approach was to understand the family's way of life and design from the inside out, arranging the plan and then clothing it with the walls and roof, rather than deciding on the overall shape and adjusting the interior to fit. The library, where Blackie worked or had business meetings, was thoughtfully placed nearest the main door and as far as possible from the nursery. The drawing-room had a **recess** to hold a piano or serve as a stage for family theatricals.

No detail was too small for Mackintosh's attention – the cupboard for table-linen was heated by a hot-water cylinder to keep it dry and the drawing-room window-seat had built-in magazine racks and a radiator concealed underneath. When he handed it over to its owner Mackintosh proudly declared: 'Here is the house. It is not an Italian villa, an English mansion house, a Swiss chalet or a Scottish castle. It is a dwelling house.'

EXHIBITIONS, COMPETITIONS AND PUBLICATIONS

Architects and designers accept that every completed project requires many **draft** designs as it **evolves**, and many schemes never get beyond the drawing board. But even plans that never happen can influence other artists when seen in exhibitions or magazines. This was certainly true of the Mackintoshes' work.

VIENNA

In 1897 a group of young Viennese artists formed a breakaway organization to promote modern art. Known as 'the **Secession**', they invited the Mackintoshes to contribute to their winter exhibition of 1900. The room-setting the

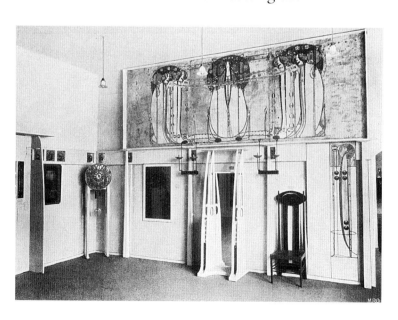

The Mackintoshes' exhibit at the 1900 Vienna Secession exhibition.

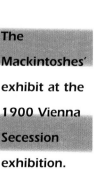

Mackintoshes put together included decorative panels, made of hessian, string and beads, which Margaret had made for one of Miss Cranston's tea rooms, and furniture they had designed for their own flat. Looking back on this first instance of recognition abroad, Mackintosh called it the high point of his life.

NO PRIZES

In 1901 Mackintosh entered a competition to design an Art-Lover's House. The competition was organized by Alexander Koch of Darmstadt, Germany, a publisher and manufacturer of wallpaper. There were 36 entries but no first prize was awarded. It would almost certainly have gone to Mackintosh if he had not broken the competition rules by failing to send three **perspective** views of his proposed interior designs. Koch did, however, award him a special prize and published Mackintosh's entry in one of his magazines.

Mackintosh's House for an Art-Lover. The symmetrical centre section contrasts with asymmetrical sections either side.

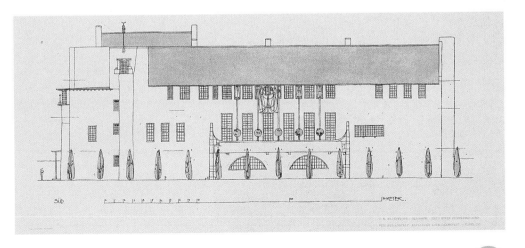

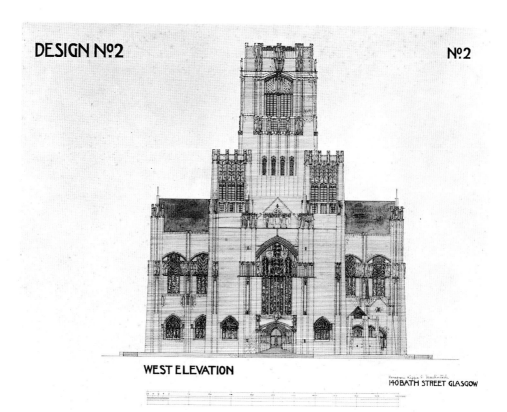

WEST ELEVATION

Hannemann Kopton & Mackintosh
140 BATH STREET GLASGOW

From drawing-board to dustbin – Mackintosh's rejected design for Liverpool Cathedral.

In the same year Mackintosh entered the competition to design a new Anglican Cathedral for Liverpool, basing his plan on the great medieval cathedral at Durham. Mackintosh's entry never even got to the second round. Mackintosh, probably wrongly, blamed the professional jealousy of one of the judges.

SUPPORT FROM FRIENDS

In 1902 the Mackintoshes' old teacher 'Fra' Newbery was put in charge of organizing the Scottish section of an International Exhibition of Modern Decorative Art, staged by the Italian government in Turin. At Newbery's invitation the Mackintoshes contributed a room-setting in white, pink, silver and green featuring roses everywhere and called 'The Rose Boudoir'. Pictures of their exhibit were published in *Deutsche Kunst und Dekoration* (German Art and Decoration), which later featured their work at Hill House.

Over the next decade the work of the Mackintoshes was to appear in other international exhibitions organized in Moscow, Dresden, Berlin, Budapest and Venice. But in Britain practical appreciation of their talent – outside the pages of **avant–garde** art magazines – remained confined to a circle of faithful supporters in and around Glasgow.

German support

In March 1902 *Dekorative Kunst* carried an article by Hermann Muthesius on the work of the Mackintoshes. It was the longest piece to appear about them in their lifetime. Concentrating on their joint work as interior decorators, rather than on Mackintosh's work as an architect, Muthesius stressed their unique talent to create rooms not just to contain works of art but to be works of art themselves. He also emphasized their ability to successfully combine opposing but **complementary** elements in Scottish tradition – from the dreamy, mystical world of **Celtic myth** and the dour harshness of the **Puritanical Calvinists** and **border chieftains**. Muthesius also devoted an entire chapter to the work of the Mackintoshes, particularly their Glasgow apartment, in his highly influential book *Das Englische Haus* (The English House), published in 1904.

THE PARTNER

Fireplace, fitted seating and stencilled walls designed by Mackintosh for the drawing-room at 14 Kingsborough Gardens, Glasgow.

In 1901 Mr Honeyman retired and Mackintosh became a **partner** in the firm of Honeyman, Keppie and Mackintosh. He was, however, very much a junior partner. As a young married man with no family fortune behind him he had to buy his share of the business in stages over a number of years. Fortunately Mackintosh's growing reputation brought him an increasing number of **commissions**, including church decorations, furniture and fittings, and a music salon in Vienna.

SCOTLAND STREET SCHOOL

In 1903 Mackintosh was appointed by the School Board of Glasgow to build a new school in Scotland Street. Its design showed the same attention to practical detail as Mackintosh had shown at Hill House. The games hall and domestic science room faced north so that they could be as cool as possible. In the cloakrooms hot-water pipes ran behind the coat hooks so that wet clothing could be dried out and warmed before the children put it on again. The grand staircase towers over the entrances have walls of glass to flood the interior with light. Infants were given their own little entrance so that they would not be jostled by the older children.

THE WILLOW TEA ROOMS

Scotland Street School.

Glasgow's main street, Sauchiehall Street, means 'alley of the willows' and this gave Mackintosh his theme for decorating Miss Cranston's Willow Tea Rooms.

Part of the pleasure of going to one of these tea rooms was to see other people and be seen by them. Mackintosh played on this by using screens and balconies to create three connected but separate apartments. Sitting in one of his high-backed chairs gave a sense of privacy, like being protected by a wall which wasn't actually there at all, seeing other people quite clearly but feeling somehow that they were not seeing you. The colour scheme **harmonized** rich purple upholstery with silver mirrors and soft grey carpets, offset by tiny touches of pink or mauve on doors or windows. The walls were covered with panels of white plaster and leaded glass. A local newspaper praised the overall effect as 'simply a marvel of the art of the upholsterer and decorator'.

In 1906 Mackintosh added a 'Dutch kitchen' to Miss Cranston's Argyle street premises. Apart from the tiles in the fireplace there was little that was Dutch about it. The main **motif** was a black-and-white chequer pattern, appearing in varying sizes. The only splashes of colour were the bright green Windsor-style chairs and a touch of pink in the one window. The overall effect was dark and cosy, quite unlike his previous schemes which played with light and relied on bold, swirling shapes and patterns.

Whereas Mackintosh's other projects were intended for particular groups of people – students or schoolchildren, a congregation of worshippers or the residents of a house – the tea rooms were open to anyone who cared to come in, giving thousands of people the chance to look at and experience 'the Mackintosh style'.

The Salon de Luxe at the Willow Tea Rooms.

THE BEGINNING OF THE END

By 1906 the Mackintoshes could afford to buy, rather than rent, a home. They chose a three-storey end of terrace house, built in the 1850s. Almost six months was spent altering and decorating it to their taste. The ground-floor dining-room was dark, reflecting their belief that a candle-lit table, sparkling with silver and glass, should be the main focus. The first-floor drawing-room, by contrast, was an explosion of light, thanks to the long, south-facing window they had put in.

LOSING HIS WAY

In 1906 Mackintosh was elected a Fellow of the Royal Institute of British Architects, recognizing his position as a leading member of the profession. But, just when he might be expected to have gone from strength to strength, his career began to falter.

In one of his public lectures Mackintosh had argued that any real artist must be prepared to struggle for his or her art and if necessary to put up with misunderstanding and even ridicule. In 'Fra' Newbery, Miss Cranston, William Davidson and Walter Blackie, Mackintosh had found supporters who believed in his talent. But such **patrons** were not easy to find. In 1906 Mackintosh agreed to build a house at Killearn, Stirlingshire, in whatever style the client wanted, which turned out to be a Cotswold stone manor-house. Mackintosh's design was perfectly competent but obviously the work was of little interest to him. Every time he visited the site he spent most of his time drinking in the local public house. In the end another architect was appointed to finish off the project.

Only the door hints at the unusual interior of the Mackintoshes' house.

THE SCHOOL OF ART EXTENDED

Mackintosh's powers of invention were, however, by no means dead. In 1907 he submitted plans – late – for an extension to the Glasgow School of Art. Its central core was a library whose complex woodwork and furniture show just how much Mackintosh had absorbed from the craft techniques of Japan. Three massive windows, 25 feet high, flood the interior with light. Mackintosh also designed special box-like light-fittings which directed light downwards onto individual study-spaces. Nowadays the Glasgow School of Art is regarded as Mackintosh's masterpiece and a work of genius. But when it was completed in 1909 many Glasgow folk thought it looked very odd indeed.

Mackintosh's library at the Glasgow School of Art.

THE FIRM IN CRISIS

The amount of business coming into the **practice** halved in 1910 and halved again in 1911. Mackintosh's only major **commissions** were **refurbishments** for Miss Cranston's tea rooms. According to people who worked with him at the time, Mackintosh would often go to lunch at one and drink the afternoon away, not returning until just before the office closed at five. He needed the routine and discipline of coming to work – but could no longer find work to do.

Strong natural lighting contrasts dark wood and light textiles.

THE TURNING-POINT

Mackintosh's only architectural work in 1912 was a ladies' hairdressers and minor alterations to some houses. But, even though he could scarcely plead pressure of work, when a competition was announced to design a huge new teacher training college, Mackintosh failed to go beyond producing a few vague sketches. As the deadline drew nearer the responsibility for designing the firm's entry was simply passed over to someone else.

RESIGNATION

In June 1913 Mackintosh resigned his partnership. His relations with Keppie had never been particularly good. Keppie may well have resented Mackintosh's clearly superior talent as a designer. As the firm's main organizer he was doubtless irritated by Mackintosh's **perfectionism** which often led to delays, cost over-runs and arguments with clients. And Keppie's sister, Jessie, had a longstanding **grievance** against Mackintosh. She had once hoped she might marry him, and believed he had dropped her in favour of Margaret.

FRUSTRATION

After leaving the partnership Mackintosh made a half-hearted attempt to go it alone. He missed the

*A simple square **motif** in varying sizes makes a complex effect.*

routine of the office but made no effort to set one up, preferring to work at home. Walter Blackie called round – 'I found Mackintosh sitting at his desk, evidently in a deeply depressed frame of mind. To my enquiry as to how he was keeping and what he was doing he made no response. But presently he began to talk slowly and **dolefully**. He said how hard he found it to receive no general recognition; only a very few saw merit in his work and the many passed him by ... He was leaving Glasgow, he told me ... I never saw Mackintosh again.'

GOING SOUTH

In 1914 the Mackintoshes settled in Walberswick, on the Suffolk coast. Mackintosh painted **watercolours** of flowers for a book to be published in Germany. When war broke out with Germany and Austria in August 1914, the planned book had to be shelved. War also cut Mackintosh off from his greatest admirers, in central Europe, who might have saved his career.

Unfortunately war also brought spy scares, even to sleepy Suffolk. Mackintosh's solitary life and strange accent made local people suspicious. In May 1915 soldiers raided his lodgings and found letters to

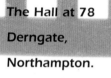

The Hall at 78 Derngate, Northampton.

artists in Vienna. Mackintosh was ordered to leave the east coast, where a German invasion was thought most likely.

LONDON

In August 1915 the Mackintoshes settled in neighbouring studios in Chelsea, London. Drawings surviving from this period show Mackintosh's designs for a block of shops and offices, a warehouse, a fountain, lamp **standards** and a war memorial. None came to anything. Thanks to the war, big architectural projects were impossible. But the war was good for engineering firms. In 1916 the engineer Wenman J. Bassett-Lowke asked Mackintosh to alter, redecorate and furnish a narrow, terraced house he had bought in Northampton. Mackintosh was inspired and transformed 78 Derngate into a stunning residence.

Transformation

Mackintosh's transformation of 78 Derngate in Northampton was a minor miracle. He put a bay window on the dull street front. He turned the staircase sideways, changing a tiny front parlour into a hall doubling as a lounge and making space for a pantry and bathroom. Adding a three-storey bay to the back enlarged the basement kitchen and dining-room and gave balconies to two bedrooms. The ingenious alterations were matched by dramatic decorations, contrasting black walls, screens and **lacquered** furniture with bright **stencilled** panels of bold, triangular patterns.

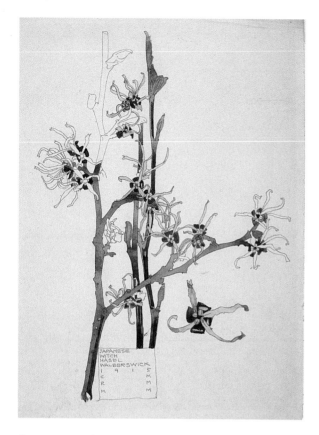

Mackintosh's only other war-time project was the Dug-Out, a basement addition to Miss Cranston's Willow Tea Rooms. Back in Chelsea both he and Margaret designed **textiles** to bring in cash they badly needed. Apart from that Mackintosh spent his time on **watercolours** of flowers and designing sets and costumes for The Plough, a local theatre group.

Japanese witch hazel painted in a Japanese style.

DESIGNS FOR DISAPPOINTMENT

By the war's end Mackintosh was reduced to begging William Davidson of Kilmacolm to buy a picture so that he could pay his outstanding rent and taxes. In 1920 things finally seemed to look up when a large building-plot became available in Glebe Place, where Mackintosh lived. Within the year artistic friends asked him to design three neighbouring studio houses, a block of apartments and a small theatre. But money and planning problems meant that only one was ever built – painter Harold Squire's studio house at No. 49. And he moved out two years later after seeing a ghostly rider. (A horse, buried on the site, was found during building.)

Designing textiles still brought in a trickle of money. Publisher Walter Blackie **commissioned** some designs for leaflets and book covers. But, frustrated by the failure of his Chelsea projects, Mackintosh became increasingly depressed. The last entry in his office diary, 13th January 1921, recorded the purchase of three pencils and two bottles of ink – but no project to use them on. Perhaps it was time to move again.

Hours on this clock are marked by 1 to 12 tiny holes.

RETIREMENT AND REMEMBRANCE

With no major project to work on Mackintosh became frustrated and depressed. J. D. Fergusson suggested a long holiday in the sunshine. In 1923 the Mackintoshes left London for southern France where they could live cheaply. What began as a long holiday stretched into a four-year stay. Mackintosh at last accepted that his career as an architect was over and chose to devote himself to an old and constant passion – **watercolour** painting.

In France Mackintosh painted both flower studies and dramatic landscapes.

After moving from one modest hotel to another the Mackintoshes finally settled in the winters at the Hotel du Commerce at Port Vendres. In the summers they retreated inland to the mountains, where it was cooler and even cheaper to live. Money was a real problem. When Margaret went to London for medical treatment in 1927, Mackintosh was wretchedly lonely without her. To save on postage he would wait until he had filled five sheets – the most that could be sent for the cheapest stamp – before sending off each letter. Margaret, meanwhile, tried to sell some of her husband's flower paintings to *Homes and Gardens* magazine.

FLOWERS AND LANDSCAPES

Mackintosh, who painted outdoors most of the time, appreciated the fine climate and also enjoyed the good French food and wine. The bright colours and harsh, rocky landscape of the region fascinated him but he felt no need to paint it exactly as it was. When picturing the village of Palalda, for example, he left out buildings he disliked and changed the colour of the roofs. Mackintosh was less interested in recording a view than in re-designing it to his taste. He worked slowly at his watercolours, finishing only about 40 in all. Both his flower pictures and his landscapes were painted in fine detail. A picture could take up to three weeks and when the weather was bad nothing got done.

No Happy Ending

Mackintosh intended to do enough watercolours for a show in London. But it was not to be. After complaining that French tobacco blistered his mouth he returned to Britain for treatment and was diagnosed as having cancer of the throat and tongue. In 1928 he went into hospital for painful **radium** treatment. For a few months he was well enough to sit out under a tree in the garden of a rented house in Hampstead. He died, aged sixty, on 19 December 1928 and was cremated at Golders Green Cemetery in north London. Margaret went back to France each year for the summer and died five years later.

Mackintosh at 52 – and looking even older.

CHARLES RENNIE WHO ... ?

In 1929 a group of Austrian architects, after tracking down an address for Mackintosh, invited him to Vienna so that they could honour his influence on the art and architecture of their country. They did not even know that their hero had died.

After Margaret's death the entire contents of their Chelsea studio were valued at £88. A large collection of Mackintosh's drawings and 31 of his paintings were listed as being 'practically of no value'. Four of the remarkable chairs Mackintosh designed were valued at £1. Just over 40 years later a single Mackintosh chair would be sold at auction for £9,300!

A meeting room at the Glasgow School of Art.

STILL STANDING

Although some of Mackintosh's buildings have been demolished most are still standing, some have been restored and a number are open to visitors. Hill House in Helensburgh is now owned by the National Trust for Scotland and open to visitors, who can see an audio-visual programme about the architect's life. The gardens are being restored to Mackintosh's original design.

Chair and bed from Hous'hill, Glasgow, home of Miss Cranston.

Public buildings in Glasgow

- The Glasgow School of Art, now recognized as one of Mackintosh's greatest works, is still an art school.
- The Willow Tea Room at 217 Sauchiehall Street has been partly restored to his original design but most of it is now a jeweller's.
- Queen's Cross Church at 870 Garscube Road is now the headquarters of the Charles Rennie Mackintosh Society, with its own information centre, reference library and bookstall.
- Scotland Street School is now a Museum of Education, illustrating the changes in school furniture and equipment since Mackintosh's day.
- Craigie Hall at 6 Rowan Road contains a music room and library incorporating Mackintosh designs.
- The premises of the *Glasgow Herald* are at 68-76 Mitchell Street and those of the *The Daily Record* are at 20-28 Renfield Lane.
- Other surviving Mackintosh exteriors include Martyr's Public School, Ruchill Church Hall and the Ladies' Art Club.

FURNITURE AND INTERIOR DESIGN

Mackintosh furniture can be seen in the main Glasgow Museum and Art Gallery in Kelvingrove Park and in the Hunterian Art Gallery in Hillhead Street. The Hunterian collection includes a reconstruction of three floors of the now demolished home at 6 Florentine Terrace where the Mackintoshes lived between 1906 and 1914. The rooms show all the alterations and improvements they made to the original house, together with some from their flat at 120 Mains Street.

The Glasgow School of Art has furniture from Windyhill and several of Miss Cranston's Tea Rooms. Other public collections containing work by Mackintosh include the British Museum, Tate Gallery and Victoria and Albert Museum in London, the Scottish National Gallery of Modern Art in Edinburgh, Northampton Museum, Brighton Museum and Graves Art Gallery in Sheffield. Overseas Mackintosh is represented in collections in Paris, Vienna, Trondheim, New York and Richmond, Virginia.

MACKINTOSH REBORN

Since 1973, when the University of Glasgow granted them the legal right, the Italian firm Cassina has reproduced furniture in Mackintosh designs. They began with four chairs and expanded the list to twenty different items, all faithfully reproduced to his **specifications**. The Mackintosh **copyright** expired 50 years after his death, so since 1978 the 'Mackintosh' style has been borrowed in the design of clocks and cutlery, tiles and **textiles**, light-fittings and lampshades. Many of these items are packaged and marketed with 'Mackintosh' lettering, despite the fact that he never designed a whole alphabet.

Mackintosh is unlikely to have approved the greedy abuse of his ideas but he would surely have been flattered by the construction in 1992 of an Artist's

Cottage at Farr, near Inverness, based on a design of his, prepared in 1900 but never built. Even more pleasing would be the knowledge that the Art-Lover's House he submitted for the 1901 Darmstadt competition has now been built at Bellahouston Park, Glasgow, as an international study centre for **architecture** and the visual arts.

A Mackintosh chair manufactured by Cassina of Milan.

CHARLES RENNIE MACKINTOSH – OPINIONS

'… if one were to go through the list of truly original artists, the creative minds of the modern movement, the name of Charles Mackintosh would certainly be included even amongst the few that one can count on the fingers of a single hand.'   Hermann Muthesius, German architect, diplomat and personal friend, 1902

'No artist owes less to tradition than Charles Rennie Mackintosh: as an **originator** he is supreme.'
J.Taylor, art critic, 1906

'The whole **modernist movement** in European **architecture** looks to him as one of its chief originators.'
Obituary of Charles Rennie Mackintosh, *The Times*, 1928.

'… the European counterpart of Frank Lloyd Wright and one of the few true forerunners of the most ingenious juggler with space now alive: Le Corbusier. Le Corbusier once confessed that his desire in building is to create poetry. Mackintosh's attitude is very similar. Building in his hands becomes an **abstract** art, both musical and mathematical.'
Professor Nikolaus Pevsner, architectural historian, 1936

The Willow
Tea Rooms
exterior
today.

'During the planning and building of the Hill House I necessarily saw much of Mackintosh and could not but recognize, with wonder, his inexhaustible fertility in design and his astonishing powers of work ... he was a man of much practical competence, satisfactory to deal with in every way, and of a most likeable nature.'

Walter Blackie, publisher and **patron**, 1943

'Employing only the finest obtainable craftsmen, accepting only the finest materials and workmanship, never hurrying, he lost money on every job he undertook, was the despair of his **partners**, and lived and died a gloriously poor man. But he **revolutionized** world architecture.'

Desmond Chapman-Huston, friend, 1947

'... no English craft furniture had the daring of that designed by Charles Rennie Mackintosh for his Glasgow buildings ...'

Marigold Coleman,
Deputy Director of the Crafts Council, 1983

'Although Mackintosh is now one of the world's most famous architects, his work was not always highly rated. He died in 1928 a neglected figure and the postwar period saw some of his most famous buildings threatened with demolition. It was not until the 1960s that his work was reassessed, and his importance as a key **transitional** figure from the **historicism** of the nineteenth century to the **abstraction** of the twentieth century acknowledged. '

Catherine McDermott,
university lecturer in design history, 1997

Mackintosh – no longer forgotten.

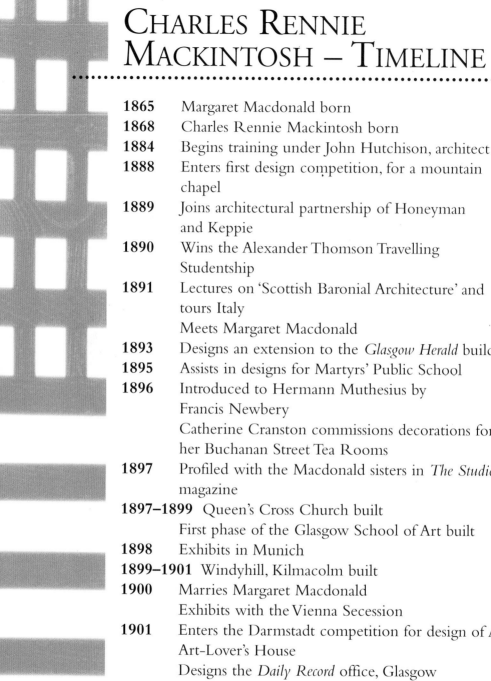

CHARLES RENNIE MACKINTOSH – TIMELINE

1865	Margaret Macdonald born
1868	Charles Rennie Mackintosh born
1884	Begins training under John Hutchison, architect
1888	Enters first design competition, for a mountain chapel
1889	Joins architectural partnership of Honeyman and Keppie
1890	Wins the Alexander Thomson Travelling Studentship
1891	Lectures on 'Scottish Baronial Architecture' and tours Italy
	Meets Margaret Macdonald
1893	Designs an extension to the *Glasgow Herald* building
1895	Assists in designs for Martyrs' Public School
1896	Introduced to Hermann Muthesius by Francis Newbery
	Catherine Cranston commissions decorations for her Buchanan Street Tea Rooms
1897	Profiled with the Macdonald sisters in *The Studio* magazine
1897–1899	Queen's Cross Church built
	First phase of the Glasgow School of Art built
1898	Exhibits in Munich
1899–1901	Windyhill, Kilmacolm built
1900	Marries Margaret Macdonald
	Exhibits with the Vienna Secession
1901	Enters the Darmstadt competition for design of An Art-Lover's House
	Designs the *Daily Record* office, Glasgow
	Becomes a partner in Honeyman and Keppie
1902	Designs Scottish section of the Exhibition of Modern Decorative Art, Turin
	Muthesius profiles the decorative work of the Mackintoshes in *Dekorative Kunst*

1902–1903	Hill House, Helensburgh built
1903	Designs decorations and furniture for Miss Cranston's Willow Tea Rooms
	Exhibits in Moscow
1906	Scotland Street School built
	Elected a Fellow of the Royal Institute of British Architects
	Moves from 120 Mains Street to 6 Florentine Terrace
1907–1909	Glasgow School of Art extended
1909	Paints flower studies at Withyam, Kent
1910	Disastrous decline in business for Mackintosh's architectural practice
1911	Designs a Cloister Room and Chinese Room at the Ingram Street Tea Room
1913	Resigns from his architectural partnership with Honeyman and Keppie
1914	Outbreak of the First World War
	Moves to Walberswick, Suffolk
1915	Settles in Chelsea, London
1916	Designs decorations and furniture for 78 Derngate, Northampton
	Designs fabrics for Liberty's and Foxton and Sefton of London
1920	Prepares designs for studios, flats and a theatre in Chelsea
1923	Moves to France
1927	Diagnosed with cancer of the tongue and returns to London
1928	Death of Charles Rennie Mackintosh
1933	Death of Margaret Mackintosh
	Mackintosh Memorial exhibition held at McLellan Galleries, Glasgow
1952	Thomas Howarth's biography of Mackintosh published
1963	Mackintoshes' home at 6 Florentine Terrace demolished
1973	Cassina of Milan begin to reproduce Mackintosh furniture
1977	Queen's Cross Church becomes headquarters of Charles Rennie Mackintosh Society
1978	Copyright of Mackintosh's designs expires
1992	Artist's Cottage built at Farr to Mackintosh designs

GLOSSARY

abstract not intended to look like a particular thing

architecture the art of designing buildings

asymmetrical when the two halves of something are not symmetrical

avant-garde new or experimental movement in art

baronial in the style of a lord or chieftain

border chieftain head of clan of warriors who raided the border lands between Scotland and England

British Empire overseas areas ruled or settled by Britain

Celtic myth ancient legends about gods and heroes of the non-English speaking peoples of the British Isles – the Scots, Welsh and Irish

champion strong supporter of a person or idea

civic of or to do with a city

cloister open-sided, covered passageway

commission order for a job or project

complementary going well together

contracted sinew part of a muscle which fails to flex properly

controversial causing an argument

copyright legal right to produce copies and control an original artistic work

decor decoration of a room or house

draft first or early sketch

dolefully sadly

draughtsman person skilled at technical drawing

enamel coloured, glasslike decorative coating on metal

evolve take shape gradually through stages

Fellow full member of a professional association

fortified strengthened for defence

Gothic architectural style of the Middle Ages, featuring pointed arches

grievance cause for complaint or resentment

harmonized blended in a pleasing way

historicism tradition relying on the ideas and examples of the past

immortal living for ever

Impressionist style of painting which aims to convey the effects of light

lacquered painted with lacquer as a decoration or protection

modernist movement group of artists who favoured new or experimental styles

motif decorative shape

originator inventor or pioneer

partner senior member of a firm entitled to a share in the profits

patron person who uses their money to support an art or artist

pavilion temporary building to house an exhibition

perfectionism demanding the highest standards

practice architect's business and network of clients

pupilage period of training as the pupil of a master

Puritanical Calvinists followers of religious teacher John Calvin who held very strict views

radium radioactive substance used to treat cancer

recess part of a room set back from the wall

refurbishment renewal of decoration or fittings

Renaissance style based on the 'Classical' models of ancient Greece and Rome

revolutionized changed completely

roughcast surfacing made of tiny stones

secession breakaway movement

specifications particular requirements

standard frame to hold up a lamp

stencilled pattern painted on using a cut-out

suburbs areas where people live, on the edges of town

symmetrical where the two halves of something are identical reflections of each other on opposite sides of a central line

tenement large block of flats

textiles woven cloth

transitional linking one period or style with the next

watercolours paintings done on paper with water-based paints

Whistler (John Abbot MacNeill) nineteenth-century American painter who settled in London, and is famous for his portraits of people and views of the Thames

INDEX